The Soul Survives
and Religion Lies

By

Ron Patterson

Dedication

Dedicated to the memory of my son, Jeff. He loved life, loved people, and hated no one. He was taken by the gay plague in the prime of his life. I hope to meet him again.

i

Author's Note

This is my second book. The first one, "A Worldview According to Evidence," written over a year ago, was a dud. Written in haste and submitted to a self-publisher whom I believe ripped me off and gave me no control over pricing. They priced the book, Kindle, and paperback, way above what the market could bear. Both should have been priced at less than half of what they were priced at. To say the book did poorly would be an understatement.

However, since almost no one read the book, I have repeated a few points I made in that book. But only a few. Also, looking back, the book was written from a different perspective. I plan to correct that problem in this book. I will be brief, using as few words as possible to convey my point. I will not try to baffle you with bullshit using sesquipedalian* words when a much shorter term would do. (*A foot and a half long.) I will write in a vernacular that any young adult can understand. Though if you are a deeply religious person, you will find some of it offensive, perhaps even shocking. If so, you may assume that was my intention.

My reasons for writing this short book are to avoid misleading anyone. I am a strong advocate of the scientific method. I believe in science though I believe science has a blind spot, which I will describe in detail later in the book. For almost all my adult life, I have called myself an atheist. However, some would label me as a deist. I wouldn't say I like that label. The word "deist," like the word "god," means something different to different people. I believe the universe was set into motion by some conscious entity. I must confess I have absolutely no idea as to the nature of that conscious entity.

Contents

Our Belief System

Premise

I am an old man, 85 years of age, and in fair health. Most would say I am a presumptuous old fool to attempt to write such a book as I now try to write. They would say that because I am not a scientist, philosopher, or a member of any profession that deals with the subjects I am about to critique. But I have studied all of them all long life. A short bio is in order. In it, I will explain why I feel qualified to embark on this attempt to critique the subjects in this book.

I was born in a three-room sharecropper's shack in 1938. I was the sixth of ten siblings, nine of whom survived to adulthood. Dirt farmers, in those days, usually had many children. Children were farmhands that only cost the farmer room and board. They also gave the farmer and his wife much love and all the heartaches and problems with raising children.

In those days, dirt farming was backbreaking labor. I hated every minute of it. In high school, I had no direction for my life. I only knew that I would not be a farmer. But luckily, a few years after I graduated from high school, and with the aid of electronics training I received in the US Air Force, I found the job I dearly loved.

Though I had no engineering degree, my job title was "Field Service Engineer." I worked for a large mainframe computer manufacturer. About twenty percent of my time was spent either on the road or repairing large mainframe computers or their peripherals. I spent the rest of the time in my office, if

I was lucky enough to be a resident engineer, or in my home, reading about my favorite subject of the day.

That subject might be astronomy, paleontology, geology, anthropology, psychology, or some other scientific "ology" subject. I wanted to know what I referred to as "the answers." By that, I mean the answers to life's mysteries. Does life have any meaning? Is there a purpose behind it all? Admittedly, I have not found all the answers. However, I believe I have found some of the answers. Here is one of the most important things my decades of research have taught me. I have discovered that there is overwhelming evidence that the material world is not all that exists.

Here I must give a brief description of "materialism." Materialism, sometimes called naturalism, is the philosophy that the universe is made up of matter and energy and nothing else. Materialists deny the existence of anything non-material, like telepathy, clairvoyance, precognition, or any type of extrasensory perception. And they certainly deny the existence of life after death.

That our belief system is deeply flawed is not some harebrained theory I came up with on my own. I discovered it is also the opinion of almost everyone who ever investigated the science of epistemology.

Skepticism as a Belief System

I have about two dozen books in my library on why we believe what we believe or dealing with that subject. Most of them, unfortunately, are wordy and tedious, taking ten or more pages to say what could be said in one. The titles of just a few of them are "How We Know What Isn't So, Why People Believe Weird Things, and Believing Bullshit," which are dogmatic, implying that nothing outside the material world exists.

Others are just as dogmatic but in the opposite direction, implying that they know the truth and proceed to tell you how they know what they think they know. One such book is titled "How Do We Know?" That book stated on the very first page, "This book is an introduction on epistemology that is written from a Christian perspective."

That is the case for most epistemology books. They assume a prior truth. For instance, the book "How We Know What Isn't So" by Thomas Gilovich is a book on epistemology written from a materialist perspective. However, the author does not make that specific claim. He writes in a chapter titled Belief in ESP:

> *One thing that can be said about ESP is that it compels our attention regardless of whether or not it exists. If, despite current evidence to the contrary, we should someday discover the reality of psi, then both science and everyday life would change more dramatically than even the most creative science-fiction writers have imagined. On the other hand, if*

3

ESP is nothing but an illusion that it currently appears to be, we are left with the fascinating question of why many people are convinced of its existence.

Here I must disagree with Professor Gilovich. Science deals exclusively with the physical world. ESP, if proven, would prove that the non-physical world exists. It should not affect science. As to everyday life, I cannot imagine how that would change at all, except a few people would become more enlightened on the subject.

Other books on epistemology, however, are less dogmatic. One such book, by D.B. Ramsey, is "Speaking of God: We Don't Know Shit." I loved that little book, I read it cover to cover in one sitting. But one of my favorites is titled "On Being Certain: Believing You Are Right Even When You're Not," by Dr. Robert A. Burton. Dr. Burton tells us the revolutionary premise of his book is:

> *Despite how certainty feels, it is neither a conscious choice nor even a thought process. Certainty and similar states of "knowing what we know" arise out of involuntary brain mechanisms that, like love or anger, function independently of reason.*

The certainty Dr. Burton is talking about is not the type found in mathematics, as in 2+2=4. It is the certainty we feel about our core beliefs and our worldview. Most Christians "know" that the Bible is the inspired word of God, while most atheists "know" that nothing exists except the material world. Neither arrived at this supposed "knowledge" by logic or reason. If not, how did they gain this seemingly, absolute knowledge?

In other words, how do people who are sure they possess the truth about how the world works know they are correct? Of course, they don't know that at all. They think they do. They have this feeling of knowing that no argument is sufficient to dislodge. I can think of a few rather obvious explanations that cover the vast majority of the believing world. I will discuss those here. Others require a much deeper psychological or neurological explanation. Dr. Robert A. Burton, a neurologist, does cover many of those in his book, but I am neither a psychologist nor a neurologist, so I will leave those to him and other professionals.

This short book is written neither from a religious nor materialist perspective. I believe in science. I would never argue with a scientist about provable, testable science. I would go even further. Though we can only observe the universe as it exists today, we can still calculate how it all must have begun by measuring the recession of galaxies and the cosmic microwave background radiation. I think that the Big Bang Theory is correct. And that is the opinion I will hold until a better theory comes. I doubt that will ever happen, but I can turn on a dime if that ever happens.

I stress my opinion here because I want to clarify that I am not anti-science. I am a Darwinian without any theistic beliefs whatsoever.

However, scientists sometimes drift off into belief systems that cannot be tested or supported by observation. Such theories are easy to identify because they can only be supported by faith and are, not always but quite often, vigorously opposed by other scientists.

Stating the Obvious Why We Believe

Early Indoctrination

First, and by far the most obvious reason why we have that feeling of knowing what is true and what is false about the world is early indoctrination. In most of the world, children are indoctrinated from birth in the beliefs of their parents and early role models. Almost every religious person knows this. It's even in the Bible. Proverbs 22:6 says, "Train up a child in the way he should go, and when he becomes a man, he will not depart from it." Or the Jesuit motto, "Give me a child until he is seven, and I will give you the man."

All childhood indoctrination programs are not equal. I lived for almost five years in Saudi Arabia. There, for young boys, half the school day was spent in religious instruction. Some of them, by the age of 12, had memorized the entire Koran, their holy book, which is about the size of the New Testament. Everyone is required to pray five times a day. All shops and businesses must close for about 15 minutes for prayer time. It's the law. It's all about repetition, repetition, repetition. Repetition is the cement for the brain. If any dictatorial state has complete control of all public media, schools, and the laws of the state, they can dictate the beliefs of the state and require that they be repeated as required incantations, repeatedly until they are set as if cement in the brain. Not one person in a thousand will become a disbeliever when raised in such a dictatorial environment.

Such indoctrination can be seen, to somewhat a lesser extent, in the fundamental evangelical Christian family. God is poured over everything, like ketchup over fries. Any misfortune is "God's Will." Anything not understood is "God works in mysterious ways." At every meal, everyone holds hands with the person sitting next to them, and the same identical incantation, called a prayer, is repeated. Such a family brings up their children in the way they think they should, and when they become adults, they will be religious fanatics, just like their parents.

When we object to such behavior by Christians, we are told that this is their religion and that all religions should be respected. I state emphatically that I will not respect such forced indoctrination on children, even in the name of religion. It is child abuse, pure and simple. We are told by people who should know better when we criticize any religion, such as Islam, for the way they treat women, denying them an education and forcing them to cover their bodies, even their faces, from head to toe, that this is racism. To this, I cry, "bullshit." Such people are letting their misguided respect for religion override their common sense. All human rights abuse, even in the name of religion, deserves nothing more than our outright condemnation.

Early indoctrination is, by far, the most common reason for our hard-core beliefs, even though most are not as obvious as we can observe in religious indoctrination. Our early upbringing, whether deeply religious, heretical, indifferent, or pernicious environment, will affect our belief system for the rest of our lives.

The Accepted Paradigm of Our Peers

According to several polls I have read lately by Pew Research and other surveyors; we are becoming less and less religious. Nowhere is this phenomenon more pronounced than it appears to be among the scientific community. This would obviously be a great development if this trend in scientific thinking stopped there. That is, if the past religious domination of science had simply stopped and had no further effect on scientific thinking. The now-accepted paradigm of most scientists is that if anything even remotely smacks religion, then it must be eschewed as if it were the devil himself.

An example is the case of the channeled scablands of Eastern Washington. But first, a little historical background information is in order. Until the early nineteenth century, it was believed that all the strata of the earth were the result of Noah's flood and that the earth was only 10,000 years old or younger. Then in 1795, Scottish geologist James Hutton proposed that the earth was much older. He believed that the changes in the earth's geological column were laid down, layer by layer, over millions of years. He called his theory "gradualism." Charles Lyell later popularized the concept of gradualism as geological uniformitarianism to challenge the then paradigm of catastrophism. Gradualism then became the new paradigm among nearly all geologists. All catastrophism was shunned as nothing but biblical nonsense.

This, of course, was scientific progress. Of course, biblical catastrophism, such as Noah's flood, was nonsense. But the new paradigm assumed all catastrophism as nonsense. It was

8

then accepted that all geological changes in the earth's strata, outside the occasional volcano, happened gradually over many millions of years. And anyone who doubted this obvious fact was spouting biblical nonsense.

In the early 1920s, geologist J. Harlen Bretz arrived in Spokane, Washington, to study what is now called the Channeled Scablands. The Channeled Scablands covers an area of 15,000 square miles and lay entirely above the Columbia River basalt deposits. They are called "Channeled Scablands" because they are crisscrossed by about 150 channels cut into the hard basalt bedrock called coulees. These coulees are up to 8 miles wide and as much as 400 feet deep with steep, almost vertical walls. The two largest coulees are Moses Coulee, 40 miles long, and Grand Coulee, 60 miles long. They were all carved out of basalt, one of the hardest rocks. Thick volcanic basalt, if it hardens slowly enough, hardens into hexagonal columns. This made it easier for the flood waters to break away. Nevertheless, these columns, weighing tons, were carried for many miles until the water slowed and could no longer move them.

Scattered over the flat basalt plains are huge granite boulders called erratics, some weighing several tons. And there were huge potholes, as much as 100 feet wide and up to 50 feet, carved in the solid basalt bedrock. What caused these strange phenomena? It could not have been ice because the ice age glaciers never reached this part of Washington. Bretz knew it had to have been a flood, a catastrophic flood.

In 1927 Bretz gave a presentation to the Geological Society of America in Washington, DC. Here he presented his theory that the Channeled Scablands were carved out by a gigantic flood. But the established geologists at the meeting were having none of it. This violated the current established gradualism paradigm. It smacked of religious catastrophism, and they told him so. Biblical catastrophic nonsense, they said. They maintained that the Channeled Scablands had to have been carved by the Columbia River, which was, for most of the scablands, fifty miles away. However, the floodwaters did eventually flow into the Snake and Columbia Rivers.

It took decades for the truth to be accepted by the geological community. Eventually, it was shown that an ice dam, during the last ice age, blocked the Clark Fork River in Montana, creating a lake over what is now Missoula, Montana. The lake was said to hold as much water as Lake Erie and Lake Ontario combined. The ice dam broke and dumped all that water creating the Channeled Scablands. And it didn't happen just once but as many as forty times over seven thousand years.

The data proving the catastrophic origin of the scablands were always there. But mere evidence is never enough to overturn an entrenched social paradigm among even the most scientific communities. When something is just intuitively known to be true, then there is no need to even look at any proposed evidence. Even if the evidence is pushed under one's nose and seems overwhelming, there still must be evidence to the contrary. You may have no idea what contrary evidence may exist, but you just know it does because it violates the currently accepted paradigm.

Of course, gradualism is true, as Hutton and Lyell clearly showed, and has been shown by mountains of evidence since their day. However, it was believed that this overthrew any vestige of catastrophism. Catastrophism was what religious nuts believed, and therefore modern-day geologists could have no part of it. It simply had to be rejected no matter what kind of evidence its proponents should present.

Some may think the bias to protect the current scientific paradigm is not strong. One scientist who knew its strength was the great German physicist and the father of quantum physics, Max Planck. He knew the stubbornness and vanity of those who believed they possessed the truth and would not see their opinions overturned. No person in authority wants to be proven wrong. More on that subject later.

The Rest of the True Believers

I have stated the two primary reasons why we feel certain that our worldview is the correct one. The two main takeaways are that we did not arrive at our core beliefs via critical thought. We either had it indoctrinated in us since birth, or it was the accepted belief of almost all our peers. In the latter case, we unconsciously accept the concept that our peers, many of them highly intelligent people, and if they accept a concept as being true, then it must be true.

The two above causes, or reasons, of why we hold to our core beliefs, regardless of all evidence that may be false, I would say, covers ninety percent of the adult population. Of course, that is just a wild-ass guess, as I know of no poll that would yield any information on this subject. There are other reasons people believe what they believe.

The question must be asked, why do some people believe wild conspiracy theories? Or why do people join religious cults like the Jim Jones suicide cult? Or the Heavens Gate suicide cult? Obviously, they were persuaded by a charismatic leader. But that does not answer why some people are so susceptible to following such a person. How the belief systems of these fanatical fringe works are questions that I will not attempt to answer. I will leave that to the psychologists and the neurologists. For the rest of this book, I will only deal with the two obvious ones.

Reason, Logic, and Evidence

It is my contention that some things are so blatantly obvious that anyone with an IQ above 85 can understand them. That is, if the question is examined using reason, logic, and evidence.

The problem is that those core beliefs are seldom, if ever, reached using reason, logic, or evidence. They are either indoctrinated in us from birth or simply what everyone else, whose opinions we respect, believes. It is my intention to show that most conspiracy theories, all religious beliefs, and some, but far from all, of what some scientists believe cannot stand the tests. They are either unreasonable, illogical, or without any supporting evidence.

I will conclude by presenting a worldview that can be deducted from reason and logic and supported by an overwhelming amount of evidence. Things that are denied because they violate one's core beliefs, and therefore, all evidence is denied or ignored altogether. I will start with an easy one.

Lies, Lies, Lies

What some people will believe is astonishing. Hundreds of people belong to the Flat Earth Society. A recent poll shows that flat earth believers number in the thousands. The astonishing thing is not just what the flat earthers believe. It is what they must disbelieve. They must disbelieve in all physics. They must disbelieve in the law of gravity. They must disbelieve that the Earth spins on its axis every 24 hours and rotates around the sun once a year. But here is the real kicker. They must believe that tens of thousands of people, perhaps even millions, are in on the conspiracy and are lying about everything. NASA, they say, is lying about ever sending anyone into space. All the astronauts are lying. Not one of them ever went into space. All the pictures of the global earth are fake, all photoshopped. They believe it's all lies, lies, lies.

But people do lie. And if only one person claims to witness an event that you would regard as a miracle, then you must consider David Hume's probability claim:

> *When anyone tells me that he saw a dead man restored to life, I immediately consider myself whether it may be more probable that this person should either deceive or be deceived or that the fact, which he relates, should really have happened. I weigh the one miracle against the other; and according to the superiority which I discover, I pronounce my decision, and always reject the greater miracle. If the falsity of his testimony would be more miraculous than the event he relates then, and not till then, can he command my belief or opinion.*

14

Conspiracy theories, by their very nature, must advocate that everyone involved in the conspiracy, in order to maintain the secret of the conspiracy, must be lying. Conspiracies do happen. But there is a limit as to how many people can be involved, or else the secret will escape. The horrible terrorist event of September 11, 2001, was a conspiracy. It was a conspiracy that involved 19 men in the USA and at least one in Afghanistan. That is all. No US Government official was involved in that conspiracy, not one.

Those who are mistaken about their belief often number in the millions. And they often rationalize the evidence that contradicts their belief. It is said that to "rationalize" is to make up rational lies. But the George Costanza principle states that it's not really a lie if you believe it. Even those who say the earth is flat are not lying; they really believe it. Even though you may believe bullshit does not make you a liar. However, if you believe those who present evidence that contradicts your belief or disbelief are all liars, you have a serious problem. The evidence that supports a near-spherical Earth is overwhelming. And the millions who present that evidence are not lying.

It is my contention that any core belief, regardless of how it was acquired, can be validated or invalidated by simply relying on reason, logic, and evidence. I will now examine the two primary belief systems of about half the world. I apologize to those who advocate Buddhism, Confucianism, Taoism, and other Eastern Religions for leaving them out of my critique. I am just not familiar enough with those beliefs to do them justice. I will concentrate on the Abrahamic Religions of Christianity, Judaism, Islam, and their primary adversary, the philosophy of materialism.

The question is, can the Abrahamic religious theology stand the test of reason and logic and refute all the evidence that contradicts their doctrines? Materialists have a different problem. Materialists believe the material world is all that exists. What they believe is not the problem. It is what they must disbelieve that questions the validity of their philosophy. They must disbelieve that anything outside the material world exists.

I appreciate the works of authors like Richard Dawkins, Sam Harris, Richard Carrier, and the late Christopher Hitchens. They are, or were, atheists, spreading the obvious fact that religion is a myth perpetuated by books of legends that are as much the word of God as Grimm's Fairy Tales. However, in the words of C.W. Dalton, in his book, "The Right Brain and Religion."

> *"Most atheists waste their lives battling against the unconquerable monster of religion--a monster impervious to the spears of reason, impenetrable by the bullets of logic, and insensible to even the thrust of common sense."*

Worth repeating, religion is impervious to the spears of reason, impenetrable by the bullets of logic, and insensible even to the thrust of common sense. That has always been my problem with the religion in which I was raised; it defies common sense. I told this story in my previous book, "A Worldview According to Evidence." But since hardly anyone read that book, I will tell it again here.

My dad, born in 1902, was a very religious man, a deacon in the Baptist Church. He believed every word of the Bible was literally the inspired word of God. I was in my late teens when I asked my dad about a problem bugging me. I

16

reluctantly approached my dad, sitting in his easy chair, reading a magazine. I asked, "Dad, how did them kangaroos get from Australia to over there where Noah's ark was? And how did they get back"? Dad jumped out of his chair like he had been shot from a cannon, put his finger right in my face, and literally yelled at me, "Son, that is the word of God, and that is not for you to question."

Therein lies the problem. If you include Islam, about fifty-five percent of the world's population believes the Bible is the inspired word of God. Yet almost the entire Bible defies reason and common sense. But it is useless to argue reason to a person to whom reason does not matter.

Today we know that evolution is true. We know that humans evolved from a lower-order species of great apes and that we have a common ancestor with chimpanzees. We know that the universe is over thirteen billion years old, and the earth is over four billion years old. Common sense tells us that the two creation stories recorded in Genesis 1 and 2 are just legends. We know there was never a worldwide flood that drowned every man, woman, toddler, and suckling babe on earth except for eight human beings saved on one big boat. Legend has it that every animal on earth was also drowned except those saved on that big boat Noah built.

Even more astonishing is that this book, supposedly written or inspired by God, tells us that we will burn in a fiery hell forever unless we believe this story. We must believe that because Adam ate a piece of fruit that God told him not to eat, we are, therefore, guilty of Adan's horrible sin and are destined to hell unless we believe God sent his son to save us. And you must believe this based on no reason or proof but faith alone.

This is obviously a threat and a bribe all in one declaration. Your options are to burn in hell forever or live forever in paradise. We are told that if this seems to defy reason and common sense that this is only because we do not understand the mysteries of God. After all, God works in mysterious ways.

However, we live in a day where some people simply cannot accept the proposition that the Bible must be taken literally. Many liberal Biblical Apologists have woven this sow's ear into a silk purse. No, they say, God never intended these stories to be taken literally. These new liberal apologists say those horrible biblical passages are just parables and allegories. They were written, they say, in that vernacular so the people of those times could understand. Of course, that is nonsense. They were legends, passed down verbally from generation to generation and finally recorded by scribes who literally believed they were true.

For instance, at least one apologist on YouTube has stated that though evolution is true, God may have picked two early Homo sapiens, one man and one woman, to be the first two people to possess souls. These two people he called Adam and Eve. But Homo sapiens evolved somewhere between 200,000 and 300,000 years ago. I don't think there is any way that scenario can work.

Of course, there are so many other things in the Old Testament that cannot possibly be a parable or an allegory. There is the slaughter of the boy babies and toddlers in Numbers 31. There is God telling the Israelites where to buy their slaves in Leviticus 25. There is the story of a man living for three days in the stomach of a big fish and then being vomited up alive in the first two chapters of Jonah.

Of course, in the days when ninety-nine percent of the people were illiterate, they would naturally believe such legends and myths. But these days, when over ninety-nine percent of people are literate, it is amazing that millions really believe this nonsense. But far worse than the absurdity of the Old Testament is the New Testament doctrine that you will be tortured, in burning fire, forever and forever, for the finite transgression of not believing the Jesus story. That is, you, because of the sin of Adam, deserve to be tortured unto infinity. But Jesus was sent to be a human sacrifice to save you from that torturous fate. And you must believe that story or the sacrifice does nothing for you. You must burn in hell forever because of Adam's sin. He took a bite from an apple when God told him not to do that.

It just makes you want to bang your head against the wall. How can anyone today believe such unadulterated nonsense? I mean, the bullshit cannot possibly get deeper than that. Yet, a vast religious industry depends on preachers and priests to convince their gullible herd of sheep that the story is true. However, I must stress that even these preachers, priests, and church hierarchy are not lying; they really believe all this horseshit.

I don't know about Europeans, but most Americans are totally ignorant of the Bible and religion in general. Many Americans think Joan of Arc was Noah's wife. And many think Sodom and Gomorrah were husband and wife. And almost every protestant, atheist, or non-Catholic in America or the rest of the world believes the Catholic doctrine of the Immaculate Conception refers to the conception of Jesus. It doesn't. On YouTube, I even heard Christopher Hitchens state: "First you had the Immaculate Conception, then the virgin birth." As if one follows the other.

19

No, the Immaculate Conception has nothing to do with how God got his Y-chromosome sperm into Mary's X-chromosome egg and created a holy zygote that later became the baby Jesus. I wonder how God got his sperm sample with which to impregnate Mary. The Bible leaves out those details. But I digress.

Let me tell you the story of the Immaculate Conception. I also believed that the Immaculate Conception referred to the conception of Jesus until a little over 30 years ago when I came across a book by Peter de Rosa titled "The Vicars of Christ: The Dark Side of The Papacy." There you will need to go if you wish to see the whole story; I will only give a much-abbreviated overview here. It's all about the conception of Mary, not Jesus.

Until about the middle of the twelfth century, all Christians took it for granted that Mary was conceived in original sin. The sex act always involves sin, even in marriage. Or that's what Christians believed in those days, and many still do. Therefore, the sex act, the sex act that conceived Mary, was just like all other fucks, dirty, filthy, rotten, and worst of all, sinful, just like all other sex acts.

But about half the Catholic hierarchy, the Franciscans, said that the mother of God could not have been conceived in sin. The Dominicans took the opposite side. They proclaimed that the sex act that conceived Mary was just like all other sex acts, filthy and sinful. There the battle raged for seven centuries. Pope Pius IX had enough of this infighting dividing his church, and he decided to settle the matter once and for all. On January the eighth, 1854, he spoke ex-cathedra. That means his words were infallible as if they came from God himself. The Infallible Deus read:

We declare, pronounce and define that the doctrine
which holds that the most blessed Virgin Mary, in the
first instant of her conception, by the singular grace
and privilege granted by Almighty God, in view of
the merits of Jesus Christ, the Savior of the human
race, was preserved free from all stain of original
sin. Is a doctrine revealed by God and, therefore, to
be believed firmly and constantly by all the faithful.

So, there you have it, as if from the mouth of God himself. The fucking that led to the conception of Mary was the only fucking in the history of the world that was not filthy dirty, and sinful. It was a clean fuck. It was not just clean; it was absolutely immaculate.

Atheism

If one reads many books or articles on the atheism/theism debate or watches many YouTube videos on the subject, and I do, you will discover that they are always talking about the God of the Bible. The debates are always between some Bible-thumping Christian and an avowed atheist.

The Christian now believes he has a new arrow in his quiver with which to puncture the atheist's balloon. That arrow is called the Big Bang. That is now the generally accepted theory that the universe sprang into existence. It sprang into existence, from nothing, with one sudden explosion or something like that. Therefore God, meaning the debater's particular god, Yahweh, the god of the Bible, had to be the cause of it all. Of course, he never says the god of the Bible did it. He just says "God" and leaves it at that. The god of the Bible is just implied.

Now you would think that the atheist in these debates, usually a scientist with a Ph.D. in his discipline, would see the logical fallacy in this line of reasoning. But he does not. He argues against God as depicted by the Bible as well as depicted by almost all theists. He argues only against the only type of god his theist opponent recognizes, a god that is all-powerful, all-wise, and all-benevolent. He goes on to argue that such a god cannot possibly exist because evil exists in the world. If God were all-powerful and all-benevolent, he would not allow evil. Neither would he allow catastrophes that kill innocent people. And he goes on to argue that the universe is a damn mess, that only a tiny fraction of planets in the universe can support life. That is such a damn waste of matter and energy that an all-powerful god would do a much better and more economical job of creating a universe. Therefore, he is forced to conclude that the universe did not have a creator. It just exists. It goes by two names, naturalism and materialism. Take your choice; both mean the same thing. There exists matter and energy and absolutely nothing else.

One can understand why the theist believes that anything that suggests that a god exists takes that as evidence that his God exists. There is, however, no logical reason for the atheist to make that same assumption. It's just not logical. It has to do with his core beliefs, which were never subjected to reason or logic.

All atheists grew up in a believing world. There was a church every few blocks or every few miles if he was raised in the country as I was. God was on our money, on our pledge of allegiance, and every politician or judge was sworn in with his hand on the Bible. But if he is lucky enough to get a higher education, and especially if he studies one of the sciences, he finds himself surrounded by people who just don't believe that shit anymore. Unless he was deeply indoctrinated in religious bullshit as a child or adolescent, he will find himself adapting to that same paradigm. That paradigm states that all religion is bullshit; therefore, God is bullshit.

Of course, God means different things to different people. Well, that is if you are a person who has given it a lot of deep thought and contemplation. Most people have not done that. For most people, God is the God that their parents, priest, or preacher told them about. It is a cut-and-dried dichotomy. Either the God they grew up hearing and reading about exists, or no God exists. And the current paradigm among most men and women of science is that no God exists. The only accepted view of the universe is that of materialism.

That leaves the atheist with one big problem, the existence of the universe. If there is no god or any god-like thing, then just where did the universe come from? Not to worry, science is to the rescue. Well, at least one scientist has the answer.

Make no mistake, if one can take anything from this short book, it is the fact that the entire new atheist movement, the atheism of Richard Dawkins, Sam Harris, Dan Dennett, the late Christopher Hitchens, and all those young internet atheists, or skeptics as they like to call themselves, is a rebellion against the establishment of religion and against the god as depicted by religion. They all seem to see the world as a dichotomy of religion versus materialism with no alternate position. They fail to realize that their deep hatred for religion has poisoned their ability to reason logically about the existence of anything outside the material world.

A Universe from Nothing

It is my contention, and I will try to prove logically that there are two options as to how the universe came into being. That is either some kind of conscious entity, or a god-like thing created it, or the universe just exists as "brute fact."

Philosopher Dr. Keith Parsons defines a brute fact this way: "to posit something as an ultimate brute fact is to say, inter alia, that it is not caused by, derived by, derived from, reducible to, composed of, conditioned by, an epiphenomenon of, or supervenient upon anything else."

A brute fact is something that has no explanation. It is just a brute fact and nothing else. Bertrand Russell was once asked why he thought the universe exist, and he responded, "I should say that the universe is just there, and that's all." He did not say that the universe did not need an explanation. He simply stated that the universe had no explanation.

To most people, whether religious or atheist, the universe as a brute fact is not a satisfactory explanation. To the religious, God created the universe. That is the god of their religion. To most scientists, though not all, religion is a myth; therefore, the universe must have another cause, a scientific cause. The point of contention seems always to be religion.

Can science explain how a universe can pop out of nothing? One scientist has written a book, a bestseller no less, that he believes explains how the universe did exactly that, pop out of nothing. He is Dr. Lawrence Krauss, and his book has the title "A Universe from Nothing: Why There Is Something Rather Than Nothing."

The problem with Dr. Krauss's nothing is that it is far from being nothing. Dr. Krauss's "nothing" contains lots of space, quantum laws, and lots of microscopic particles and anti-particles popping into existence, with energy borrowed from somewhere; then, in a millionth of a second or so, the particle and antiparticle recombine and annihilate each other, returning the energy to from whence it came. Or at least that is the general gist of the story. They do this because, as Dr. Krauss explains because this "nothing" is very unstable.

Of course, no one has ever seen one of these particles or antiparticles, but they say they have detected them in vacuum chambers, so they know they exist. Some say they are electrons and positrons, but no one really knows. I even read one article that said they are quarks and antiquarks. However, I think that is a real stretch.

However, the biggest stretch of all is turning these microscopic particles into a massive finely-tuned universe. From this unstable nothing, there sprang all the mass, all the energy, and all the laws of the universe. From this unstable nothing came electrons, up quarks, down quarks, neutrinos, massless particles such as gluons and photons, and the Higgs boson. But that is not all. From this unstable nothing, there had to spring all the laws, constants, and forces of the universe. Suddenly popping from this, nothing had to be gravity, the magnetic force, the strong and weak nuclear forces, dark matter, and dark energy. Then there are all the many constants and forces that govern such things as stellar nucleosynthesis. That is what creates all the elements in the periodic table, from primordial hydrogen and helium.

It must also be noted that every particle that sprang from nothing, in order that they do not violate the law of conservation of energy, had to be accompanied by its antiparticle. Even all dark matter particles, which make up eighty-five percent of all matter in the universe, had to be accompanied by an anti-dark matter particle. But all these antiparticles, for some strange reason, disappeared without taking their associated particle with them. This is still a mystery to which science has no answer.

It is just assumed that all the laws and constants that also sprang from nothing did not need an anti-law or an anti-constant. Only matter needs antimatter to be able to just pop out of unstable nothing. But what about energy? According to Dr. Einstein's equation, $E=MC^2$, matter and energy are the same things. We are told that dark energy makes up seventy percent of the total universe. How did that pop out of the unstable nothing? Did there exist anti-energy?

Dr. Krauss said in an interview with Atlantic's Ross Anderson:

> *What drove me to write this book," Krauss said of 'A Universe from Nothing,' "was this discovery that the nature of 'nothing' has changed, that we've discovered that 'nothing' is almost everything and has properties. That, to me, is an amazing discovery. So how do I frame that? I frame it in terms of this question about something coming from nothing. And part of that is a reaction to these really pompous theologians who say, 'Out of nothing, nothing comes,' because those are just empty words.*

Dr. Krauss did not inform us as to who made this discovery that the nature of nothing had changed, but there must be a Nobel Prize awaiting him or her. All this person must do is show that nothing doesn't mean nothing anymore. Nothing now means something. But if "nothing" now means "something," we now need a new word for what "nothing" previously meant.

As you might have guessed, Dr. Krauss's book, as well as his declaration that nothing really means something very specific and that something is governed by the laws of (already existing) quantum mechanics, has been loudly condemned by philosophers, science writers, and even some members of his own profession. Nevertheless, many in the new atheist movement have cheered his pop science book as if it were the greatest discovery ever made in physics.

Richard Dawkins is a biologist whom I greatly admire. I have not read all his books, but I have read most of them. But Dr. Dawkins is way out of his field. He writes a four-and-one-half page "Afterward" in Krauss's book. He praises the book to the high heavens and condemns those he sees as the opposition to Krauss's work, theologians. Of course, he wrote this "Afterward" before the book was published and was unaware of the wave of criticism coming from science journalists, philosophers, and even a few other scientists that would loudly condemn Krauss's work. Dawkins closes his "Afterward" with these words:

> Even the last remaining trump card of the theologian, 'Why is there something rather than nothing?' shrivels up before your eyes as you read these pages. If 'On the Origin of Species' was biology's deadliest blow to supernaturalism, we may come to see 'A Universe from Nothing' as the equivalent from cosmology. The title means exactly what it says. And what it says is devastating.

To which science journalist John Horgan replies in Scientific American:

Whaaaa...??!! Dawkins is comparing the most enduringly profound scientific treatise in history to a pop-science book that recycles a bunch of stale ideas from physics and cosmology. This absurd hyperbole says less about the merits of Krauss's derivative book than it does about the judgment-impairing intensity of Dawkins's hatred of religion.

Therein lies the problem. It's all about religion. Dawkins, and just about every other hardcore atheist, sees the teleological argument for the existence of God as a trump card for theologians. However, the teleological argument simply argues that the universe looks designed; therefore, the universe must be designed. It says absolutely nothing about the nature of the proposed designer. It says nothing about Yahweh, Zeus, Thor, Baal, or any other god ever dreamed up by man. Yet almost every atheist, as well as almost every theologian, assumes it does. Almost all the world is divided into two camps, a god dreamed up by man or no god at all. However, a few realize that if the universe was set into motion by some conscious entity, call it whatever you may, it has absolutely nothing to do with religion. In fact, the entire debate has been poisoned by religion. Christopher Hitchens was right when he said religion poisons everything.

In researching data for this book, on the internet, I came across an article titled: "A Philosopher of Religion Calls it Quits." The philosopher of religion was Dr. Keith Parsons. He states his reason for quitting was:

I have to confess that I now regard "the case for theism" as a fraud, and I can no longer take it seriously enough to present it to a class as a respectable philosophical position—no more than I

29

could present intelligent design as a legitimate biological theory.

Here is what Dr. Parsons says later in the article that left me screaming:

> *"In philosophy of religion, you do have this gap— either God exists or not. There's no middle ground."*

Of course, this philosopher of religion is talking about the God of religion. It is just assumed that the word "God" means the god of religion. In all such arguments, if one would substitute the word "religion" instead of God, the argument would become clearer and show the false dichotomy. "Either religion is true, or God does not exist. There is no middle ground." Of course, there is a middle ground. That middle ground is, "All religion is bullshit, but some kind of god does exist."

The Argument from Brute Fact

Now I wish to return to the brute fact argument. Suppose you lived in a world where gobs of stuff often popped out on nothing. Bob and Tom would be walking down the street, and suddenly, there popped, from apparently nowhere, a big gob of goo. It happens often on this planet.

Bob: Where did that come from?

Tom: Nowhere. It just exists. It just popped out of nothing.

Bob: Could it be designed?

Tom: No, these gobs have been analyzed by science all the way down to their tiniest particle. It is nothing but goo all the way down. Goo has no design. It's simply a brute fact.

Then one day, out of nothing, there suddenly popped a brand new 1959 El Dorado Cadillac Convertible.

Bob: Woah! That does look designed.

Tom: No, to say it was designed smells like religion. It gives theists a trump card.

Bob: But why? Why does it have to have any damn thing to do with religion?

Tom: Look, don't get religious on me. We cannot give those damn theologians any opening whatsoever. Anything that even remotely smells like religion must be opposed with every weapon in our arsenal. Besides, any kind of designer would have also had to just pop into existence as a brute fact.

31

Of course, Tom has a point. There had to be a first cause. However, that first cause could have started out eons ago as a tiny bit of consciousness that eventually, given enough time, could have changed over time into something far wiser and far more powerful. It is easier to imagine a bit of featureless goo popping into existence as a brute fact than it is to imagine a new 1959 El Dorado Cadillac popping into existence as a brute fact. I, therefore, submit that it is far more likely that this bit of consciousness came into existence from nothing than it is for this finely tuned universe, or the recipe for a finely tuned universe, to just pop into existence at the instant of the Big Bang. Whether it's a 1959 El Dorado Cadillac or a finely tuned universe, it screams out a designer.

There are many cosmologists that dispute the fine-tuning argument. They all seem to agree that the universe is fine-tuned but say that is just a happy accident. They say that if trillions of trillions of universes exist, then one of them is likely to have all the particles, laws, and constants that are just right to produce a rocky planet with all the conditions to allow life to evolve. They call this the multiverse theory.

I propose that this is preposterous. First, there must exist, as a brute fact, a multiverse-generating machine. And they claim that the laws, particles, and constants would be random. And just by sheer chance, one universe would get them all correct. That universe, they say, is the one we find ourselves in. That, of course, is an absurd hypothesis. After all, how many *possible* subatomic particles could exist that are not an up quark, a down quark, an electron, or a neutrino? Or how many *possible* massless subatomic particles could exist that are not a gluon or a photon? The answer in every case is an infinite number. If the case is getting just one of them right is one in infinity, then the case of getting two of them right in the same universe is one times infinity to the power of infinity. And so on, using infinity as a multiplier for each particle. We have not even begun with the laws or constants. There are upwards of forty of them. But before one can argue about the particles and constants being all correct as a happy accident, one must first get around the multiverse-generating machine. If it exists without a creator, then it must exist as a brute fact.

But we must get back to the fact that all these universes, or single universe if you do not buy into the multiverse hypothesis, must have been generated by some conscious entity, call it a designer or even God if you wish, or all this happened as a brute fact. This finely tuned universe just popped out of nothing without a cause. Those are your only two options. There exists no other option.

One might accept that a tiny particle, or a tiny bit of goo, could pop out of nothing. But it would be a bit of a stretch to imagine a brand new finely tuned Cadillac Convertible could just pop out of nothing. Yet it is readily accepted by most cosmologists that an even more finely tuned universe just popped out of nothing.

Of course, there are those who argue that this is a false dichotomy. They argue there are other options. But when you examine those arguments, they always wind up positing nothing but another brute fact. For instance, one internet atheist, Drew McCoy, who calls himself "The Genetically Modified Skeptic," posts a YouTube video called "The Argument for God's Existence, Tier List. In this video, he says of the teleological argument:

> *First, it makes use of a false dichotomy presenting pure chance and an intelligent creator as the only*

two possibilities when it hasn't successfully ruled out other options. There could perhaps be some purely physical rule to the universe which demands that these constants be the way they are.

First, Drew, the argument is not "pure chance or creator." The argument is "brute fact or creator." If there exists some purely physical rule that demands the constants be the way they are, then that purely physical rule must exist as created by some conscious entity, or it exists as a brute fact. There are no other options.

A Closer Look at the Birth of the Universe

Virtually all scientists agree that the universe had a beginning. They call this beginning "The Big Bang." A few suggest that there could have been something before the Big Bang, but they all agree that this, the current universe, began with what is commonly referred to as the Big Bang. That fact is not in dispute among cosmologists. Also, most cosmologists say that it all sprang from a single point they call a "singularity," a tiny point that, at the time, contained all the matter and energy we now find in the universe.

While most cosmologists agree with Dr. Lawrence Krauss, that the universe sprang suddenly, as just a happy accident, from primordial space that was boiling with the activity of particles popping in and out of existence. However, I know no other person in science who calls this space and activity "nothing." And no one, not even Dr. Krauss, has explained how these tiny particles suddenly turned into this fine-tuned universe. Tiny particles are one thing. Laws, forces, and constants are another thing altogether.

A brief look at the Big Bang timeline, according to most cosmologists. First, there was this tiny thing they called a singularity. Well, some called it that. Others insist that is not a proper description of that first bit of matter, or whatever it was. Then this tiny whatever began to expand faster than the speed of light. It became as big as a grapefruit. At this point, it was a hot, dense quark-gluon plasma, sometimes known as "quark soup."

This grapefruit size universe kept expanding and cooling as it did. Soon the quarks, with the assistants of the massless particles called gluons, came together to form protons and neutrons. Then the Higgs boson came from somewhere to give these particles mass. Then these protons and neutrons came together to form the nucleus of what would, much later, become the first atoms, hydrogen, and helium. Hydrogen, by mass, made up about eighty percent of all ordinary matter and helium the rest. Of course, in this expanding and cooling universe, there existed the four basic forces of nature, gravity, the electromagnetic force, and the strong and weak nuclear forces.

It would be almost 300,000 years before the universe cooled enough that hydrogen and helium nuclei could capture electrons and form the first atoms. Also, sometime during this period, no one knows exactly when or how dark matter came into existence. The amount of this dark matter created was five times the amount of ordinary matter made up of protons, neutrons, and electrons. And dark energy also existed, which is seventy percent of the total universe. No one knows much about dark energy either.

It would be somewhere between 300 and 500 million years before gravity pulled the hydrogen and helium together to form stars. Gravity then pulled these stars, and dark matter, together to form galaxies. There were about two trillion galaxies, and each galaxy contained billions to trillions of stars. But if any of these stars contained any planets, they were just balls of gas with no rocky core. Because, at this point, there were no heavy elements in the universe.

All that was about to change: inside stars, the force of gravity was fusing two atoms of hydrogen 2, deuterium, into helium 4. When that happens, then 0.71 percent of the total mass is

36

converted into energy. But it doesn't stop there. Heavier elements are fused into even heavier elements via a process called stellar nucleosynthesis. The force of gravity fuses elements all the way up to iron (fe26). Each fusion converts part of the element created to energy, to a lesser extent, for each step. But every element above fe26 absorbs energy when fused rather than produces energy. Therefore, all elements that are heavier than iron, like gold, silver, nickel, platinum, lead, and others. These elements can only be fused when the star explodes into a supernova.

The dust clouds we see in our galaxy are the remnants of not just one supernova explosion but many supernova explosions. These dust clouds contain all the natural elements of the periodic table. From these clouds, new stars are formed. These stars, though they are still mostly hydrogen, unlike the original first stars, contain heavy elements. Also, from these dust clouds and around these stars, satellites of rocky planets are formed. A tiny fraction of these stars, likely less than one in a billion, is in a quiet enough area of their galaxy, are just the right size, and have rocky planets in the goldilocks zone, which will allow life to evolve.

Nevertheless, a conservative estimate of the number of stars in the universe is 2×10^{23}. That's 2, followed by 23 zeros. Therefore, if only one star in every 100 billion stars has a planet where life could evolve, that would be 2 trillion planets capable of supporting life—about one per galaxy.

The universe, as we know it, did not all spring into existence at the Big Bang. It evolved over billions of years. I do not mean evolved as in biological evolution, natural selection. But change over time according to a pre-planned recipe that would eventually bring into being the universe as it exists today. Existing at the instant of the Big Bang, or shortly thereafter, was not only all the matter and energy of the universe but also the recipe for stars, galaxies, supernovas, rocky planets, and every element in the periodic table. These things would not come into existence for many millions of years later. At the Big Bang, there was obviously some planning ahead.

It's not just that all the particles, laws, and constants had to be exactly as they are, but also all the events, over half a billion years, had to fall into a sequence as they did. The fact that most of the scientific world accepts all this as just one big happy accident has to be because their deep hatred of religion has hindered their ability to use logic and reason in matters that seem to them may give credence to religion. Their logic seems to be that if it is championed by theologians, then it has to be wrong and must be denied at all costs. Theologians don't seem to realize that Big Bang cosmology in no way supports the God of the Bible or any of the other man-made gods, for that matter. It is a pity that so many in the scientific community, as well as so many other atheists, do not seem to understand that simple fact.

At this point, I consider the matter settled. A person can keep explaining that for this extremely fine-tuned universe to pop out of nothing, or to exist as a brute fact, violates all reason, logic, and common sense. But that would not dent the deeply held paradigm that to admit such a thing would give aid and comfort to the enemy, that is, religion, and must be vigorously opposed at every opportunity. So, we must carry on even as the cosmological community battle religious nonsense with even more nonsense of their own. I have heard that cosmologists are often in error but never in doubt.

Here I must make one thing clear. I believe in science. I am a Darwinian who accepts that all life on earth evolved from some form of nonlife billions of years ago. I believe that cosmologists are right about the Big Bang. However, if further evidence were discovered that cast doubt on the Big Bang, then I would accept such evidence for whatever it could prove. There is no evidence for the multiverse or the even more absurd many-worlds theory. There is no evidence to support the harebrained theory that something is really nothing or that the Big Bang that produced this fine-tuned universe sprang from nothing.

I repeat, there are only two options. Either this fine-tuned universe is just a happy accident that popped out of nothing for no reason, or it was created by some kind of conscious entity. You may call it God, but I dislike that title. It suggests a being to be worshipped. The desire to be worshipped is the vainest of all human emotions and highly unbecoming of some being wise enough and powerful enough to create the universe. Philosopher Dr. Jason Waller, author of the excellent book "Cosmological Fine-Tuning Arguments" makes the argument that some "god-like thing" was likely the author of the universe. I like that term. It suggests some being powerful and wise but not vain and vindictive, as is almost every god ever dreamed up by ancient mythmakers.

If some kind of god-like thing created the universe, and I do believe it was, what shall we call it? Author Nanci Danison suggests "Source." Since this god-like thing is the source of all that we know exists, that name seems appropriate. I am not entirely satisfied with that title, but I dislike the name "God" or even "the deity," and since there is no pronoun for a genderless being, I will use it. I greatly admire Ms. Danison's work. I agree with most of what she writes.

However, I have never read anyone with whom I agree one hundred percent. But she said, "My religion lied to me," that I believe.

Nanci is a former Catholic who had a near-death experience that dramatically altered her opinion of religion. She stated in a YouTube video: "What's the one true religion? There is no one true religion. They all have kernels of truth in them, wrapped up in many layers of myth, superstition, and wishful thinking."

Obviously, she is trying to be kind to religion with that definition. I will not be so kind. I like Mark Twain's definition better: "(The Bible) has noble poetry in it...and some good morals and a wealth of obscenity, and upwards of a thousand lies."

Theologians like to tell us that nothing can exist without a cause. Therefore, the universe had to have a cause. Perhaps, but a cause does not imply a purpose. A simple accident would have a cause but not necessarily a purpose. From what we can glean from the Bible and most of its believers, we must assume God created the universe, with over two trillion earth-like planets, assuming one per galaxy, to create on one of those planets creatures that looked exactly like him, in order to have them love and worship him forever. And for those that refused to do so, he would burn them in his torture chamber forever.

But I will argue that some kind of universal consciousness must be responsible for the universe. Those who believe this fine-tuned universe just popped out of nothing or believe it is either the god of religious fanatics or no god at all have let their hatred of religion cloud their logical reasoning ability.

40

I cannot make an argument powerful enough to fix that. So, I must move on.

There Must Have Been a Purpose

Some have suggested that life is so complicated that it suggests intelligent design. I vehemently disagree. I have no need for that hypothesis. However, I might consider an intelligent designer if science had not provided us with a far better answer. It's called evolution. Darwin called it "natural selection." Or, as philosopher Herbert Spencer phrased it, "survival of the fittest."

Only life can evolve. Inanimate matter cannot evolve via natural selection. One chunk of matter cannot be fitter than another. Of course, the universe did change over time, but not via survival of the fittest. The universe changed over time according to a pre-subscribed recipe that must have existed from the first instant of creation. Sub-atomic particles were created to be the substance of matter and gravity was created in order to pull them all together. Matter and energy, the recipe for it all, was there from the beginning.

I have been a science geek all my adult life. Since my early twenties, I have called myself an atheist. But that only implies that I am an anti-theist. In the late eighties, in Huntsville, Alabama, I started a monthly discussion group called "The Freethought Forum." We were loosely affiliated with The Freedom from Religion Foundation. Other members of that group never knew that, even during that time, I was a closet mystic. In fact, I have been a mystic all my adult life, or call it a spiritualist if you will, both in and out of the closet.

Being a mystic and a strong believer in science means I am a dualist. There are two basic theories of the nature of things. As I described earlier, there is materialism, and the other is dualism. That is the belief that there are two worlds, the material world, and the spiritual world. There are some who believe that only the spiritual world exists and that the material world is just an illusion. Perhaps, but I can only cover so much territory in such a short thesis. So, I will not engage those who believe that only the spiritual world exists in this book. At this point, I will just call myself a dualist. That does not mean I totally disagree with the spiritual-only world. I am just saying I will not engage in that argument today.

Materialists Dogmatism

The dictionary definition of dogmatism is "the tendency to lay down principles as incontrovertibly true, without consideration of evidence or the opinions of others." And believe it or not, we all hold some beliefs as dogma. I am guilty of holding some beliefs as dogma, and so are you. For instance, I believe the earth is a globe, not flat. I also believe the earth is billions of years old, not only a few thousand years old as the Young Earth Creationists believe. Here is the most important point about a dogma, any dogma; however, I will use my dogmatic beliefs as an example: "Any evidence that contradicts our dogmatic beliefs will be ignored."

If you present me with evidence that you believe proves the earth is flat, if I consider it at all, it will be purely for its amusement value. The reason is clear. I have already examined the overwhelming evidence that the earth is a globe and am totally convinced by that evidence. The same goes for the ancient earth and ancient universe. I have examined the geologic evidence of ancient Earth, the fossils, and the geological strata that prove beyond any doubt that the age of the Earth is billions of years. And here is another reason I will ignore your so-called evidence: I know your reasoning is based on biblical dogma, not science, and therefore is, by definition, bullshit.

If you read books written by materialists or watch many of their debates on YouTube videos, you will notice the debate is always "materialism vs. theology." That translates, in their mind, as "science vs. religion." Materialists know that religion is bullshit. They know that there was never a worldwide flood, there was never an Adam and Eve, and there was never a six-day creation as depicted in the Bible. The materialists have already examined the evidence presented by theism and found it to be totally fallacious. Therefore, any evidence presented that denies materialism is evidence for theism and need not even be examined because they know, with absolute certainty, that theism is wrong.

Conclusion: For the materialist, contrary evidence doesn't matter. No need to examine it or even acknowledge any evidence exists at all.

The guiding principle for all belief systems and worldviews should be evidence. If you feel the evidence supports your theory or hypothesis, then you should promote your theory or hypothesis. However, it should be abandoned if evidence cannot support your hypothesis.

Since I have already expressed my disdain for materialism, I will devote the remainder of this book to spiritualism, or the spiritualist side of dualism, and its supporting evidence.

I will be the first to admit that the world is full of charlatans who claim psychic powers when they have none. In fact, they are the problem. If you find one rotten apple in the barrel, it is often assumed that they all are rotten. Astrology is the perfect case. Astrology is one hundred percent bullshit. There is no evidence whatsoever that the position of the planets, or what astronomical house they are in, at the moment of your birth has any influence over your life whatsoever. Of course, astrologers, even those who write your daily horoscope for the newspaper, manage to convince themselves that they are dispatching useful information. It is really to fool yourself when you believe bullshit.

Of course, there are other charlatans that know they are phony. Many make a good living practicing the trade of "fortune telling", or telling gullible people what they wish to hear. Now some practitioners of this trade may have some talent, but most do not. I know of no way of telling them apart. But if they have a street-side parlor where they give readings with a shingle hung over the sidewalk, it's a pretty good bet that they are phony.

However, everyone is not faking it. It is just assumed, by materialists, that there is no such thing as the non-physical world. They assume that everyone who claims to have had a near-death experience is either disillusioned or lying. This includes at least ten million people in the United States alone and far more in Europe. Many tell of witnessing events and conversations that they could not have otherwise known. Many even believe that it has been proven, beyond any shadow of a doubt, that the non-physical world does not. For instance, physicist, Dr. Sean Carroll, has written a book titled, "The Big Picture: On the Origins of Life, Meaning, and the Universe Itself." In praise of that book, Dr. Steven Pinker writes:

> Sean Carrol's lucid "The Big Picture" reveals how the universe works and our place in it. Carroll, a philosophically sophisticated physicist, discusses consciousness without gimmicks, and deftly shows how the current physics is so solid that it rules out ESP forever.

Dr. Pinker believes Dr. Carroll has proven that the non-physical world does not exist because the laws of the physical world prohibit it. I am more than a little shocked that Dr. Pinker cannot see the obvious logical fallacy in that assumption. Obviously, if the non-physical world exists, then it exists outside the physical world and would not be affected by the laws of the physical world.

Near-Death Experiences

If we assume, and I do, that some kind of conscious entity, or Source as I will now call it, had to put everything in motion, then I think it logical to assume that this god-like thing, the Source, had a purpose. I will not speculate on what that purpose might have been. But others have, and many of them seem to agree on what that purpose was. Most believe we are part of the creator or God, and we are doing it for the experience. After all, if before the universe existed, there was just a void, then just existing in a void is not very exciting. But now I would like to discuss the evidence. That is, the evidence that the material world is not all that exists.

There are several ways of gathering supporting evidence of psychic phenomena, reincarnation, near-death experiences, deathbed visions, and life after death. I will discuss some of these later. I cannot do all of them justice in this short book as there have been many very good books written on each.

I will start with near-death experiences. The very respectful and popular publication Psychology Today describes such an event:

> *A near-death experience (NDE) is the conscious, semi-conscious or recollected experience of someone who is approaching or has temporarily begun the process of dying—for example, during a cardiac arrest that is followed by resuscitation. People who recall near-death experiences have described perceiving a variety of surreal phenomena, such as seeing themselves from above or passing through a tunnel of light.*

There have been many books written on NDEs, and I would guess well over one hundred YouTube videos on the subject. They are so common now that it is likely that every doctor and nurse in the nation is well familiar with them. Just how common are NDEs? The Psychology Today article goes on to say:

How common are NDEs?

Estimates vary, with some suggesting that as many as 10 to 20 percent of people who have been declared dead have had a near-death experience. In one study of patients who had survived cardiac arrest, 9 percent of survivors who could be interviewed reported an NDE.

Okay, let's do the math. I just did an internet search on "How many people have had a near-death experience?" The answer I got was 10 to 20 percent. I would rather be conservative and cut that to only 5 percent. That would mean that, just in the USA, over 16 million people have had a near-death experience (NDE). And reports out of Europe put the number at least as high there.

People have NDEs for many different reasons. Some have them after a serious accident. Others experience an NDE after violent and near-fatal allergic reactions to some drug or other medical injection. Survivors of cardiac arrest often experience a near-death experience.

Atheists have NDEs, Evangelicals have NDEs, and Catholics have NDEs. Many who experience an NDE have never heard of NDEs before they experience one. However, they are becoming more widely known. They seem more prevalent now than in the past because more people near death are being resuscitated due to better knowledge and better resuscitation equipment. There are other reasons like the internet. There are hundreds of YouTube videos about NDEs.

Dr. Raymond Moody coined the term "Near Death Experience" in 1975 in his book "Life After Life". Still, as little as 25 years ago, few people had ever heard of the term or the concept. Now almost everyone has. This has, in turn, caused thousands of people who have had an NDE to be able to discuss their experience with friends and family without them thinking they were nuts.

Many books have been written on the subject, far more than I have been able to read, but I have read many of them. Many of the books were written by medical doctors who, after so many of their patients told them stories of their experiences, they just had to tell the world about it. Of course, the first was Dr. Raymond Moody, who wrote the first book on the subject in 1975. Two of my favorites are "After: A Doctor Explores What Near-Death Experiences Reveal about Life and Beyond," by Dr. Bruce Greyson, and "Near Death in the ICU: Stories from Patients Near Death and Why We Should Listen to Them," by Dr. Laurin Bellg. Dr. Bellg tells the story of a man who had an NDE while in the ICU. He explains that he was out of his body and felt himself rising up and bumping against the ceiling. Then he rose through it, seeing wiring and pipes between the ceiling and the floor above. Then he gave this detail of what he found in the room above the ICU:

> *"It looked like a hospital, but it was different," he said pensively. "It was very quiet, and it seemed like no one was there. There were individual rooms and all around the edge and on some of the beds were these people, except they were not people, exactly.*

They looked like mannequins, and they had IVs hooked up to them but they didn't look real. In the center was an open area that looked like a collection of workstations with computers," he said.

This floored Dr. Bellg as well as the nurse who witnessed the story. That was exactly what was on the floor directly above the ICU. It was a nurse's training area with simulated hospital rooms with medical mannequins on some of the beds. And in the center was a collection of workstations with computers.

There are many other such stories in Dr. Bellg's book as well as in Dr. Greyson's book. That are situations that would have been impossible if they just came from the patient's mind. Things that had to be witnessed directly and not just figments of someone's mind while they lie comatose in a hospital bed, on the operating table, or at the scene of an accident. Dr. Greyson adds:

Some two-thirds of those having an NDE meet another person — often a dead loved one. What's especially strange is that sometimes experiencers "meet recently deceased people who were not known to have died."

NDEs are not flawless. They are highly subjective. Dr. Bellg explains:

[B]ecause our culture deeply influences our experience of life; it makes complete sense to me that it would also influence our experience of death. These powerful images are part of our rituals of shared grief and may be part of our collective experience that can comfort us at the passing of our loved ones.

50

Because NDEs are subjective and deeply influenced by our culture, very religious people will often see, in their NDE, beings whom they interpret as religious figures. Many think they see Jesus, a figure who very likely never existed. Or at least a being who never existed as he is depicted in the Bible. I must add that this is my opinion and not necessarily the opinion of any author I mention in this book.

The point is that millions of people have had an NDE or an out-of-body experience. There are thousands of such cases, like those reported by Dr. Greyson and Dr. Bellg that report witnessing things that were impossible to witness from their comatose body. That leaves the explanation that their NDE was just the result of oxygen deprivation in the brain invalid.

Again, millions have experienced an NDE. And a high percentage of them, like the one witnessed by Dr. Bellg above, cannot be explained in any way except that they happened exactly as reported. That leaves us with only two possible explanations. Either they actually happened as reported, or Europe or all those who experienced them, and all who report witnessing them, many of them doctors and nurses, are all just lying about it.

If you have a belief system that requires many thousands who claim to have evidence to the contrary to be simply lying about that evidence, then your belief system, like that of the flat-earthers, is without any validity whatsoever.

Reincarnation

Reports of near-death experiences are far more numerous than just a few years ago. There are two reasons for this. The first is far more people survive near-death encounters than just a few years ago. Although the survival of cardiac arrest is still quite low, it is far higher today because of quicker response by emergency units, better training, and better equipment. The same goes for accidental near-death encounters. Better and quicker emergency response teams greatly improve the chances of someone surviving a serious accident than just half a century ago. But there is another reason. It is no longer a taboo subject.

Today, far more people are willing to share their NDE with family, friends, and loved ones than just a few years ago. Half a century ago, the average person in America as well as in many other parts of the world, was far more religious than today. And even those who are religious are, in general, far more receptive to discussing the concept of NDEs than just a few years ago. However, while that is true for NDEs, that is not yet true for reincarnation.

While acceptance for reincarnation is far more prevalent than just a few years ago, it has not yet reached the level of acceptance of NDEs. Nevertheless, because it is no longer the taboo subject it once was, we are seeing far more reported cases in the last few years. However, reports of children remembering a previous life in America or Europe are less frequent than in many Asian countries where reincarnation is part of their religious belief system. Major Asian religions that accept the concept of reincarnation are Hinduism, Jainism, Buddhism, and Sikhism.

I suspect that the cases of children remembering a past life are just as frequent in North and South America as well as Europe is every bit as frequent as in places where it is the accepted belief. But when, in a Christian family, or even an atheist family, when a child starts to talk about his "other mommy", he is told to "shut up and stop talking nonsense. I am the only mommy you have." Nevertheless, Jim Tucker of the University of Virginia School of Medicine Department of Perceptual Studies, says they have on file 2,700 documented cases of children who talk about a previous life. Most of these cases come from Asia, where the late Ian Stevenson spent some forty years studying and documenting those cases. They have over 100 published American cases, which keeps increasing yearly.

Almost all cases follow a similar pattern. A child will start talking about his or her former life just as soon as they are able to talk. If prodded by their parents, they will give many details of that life, like where they lived, family members, and in almost all cases, how they died. The memories start to fade at about the age of five, and by the time they are seven or so, the memories are completely gone. There are a few exceptions where the memories last longer, but those are the rare exceptions.

There are many verifiable cases of reincarnation. That is where former family members are still alive and named, and places where the person lived in their former life can be checked. And past events described can be verified historically. Jim Tucker and the late Ian Stevenson have over 2,700 such cases on file at the University of Virginia, Department of Perceptual Studies. Dr. Tucker and Dr. Stevenson have written books describing many of these cases. It is important to note that Dr. Stevenson, in his over

40 years of research in the study of reincarnation, concentrated his studies on the *verification* of each case he studied. Obviously, he knew that just reporting such cases was not enough, but each case had to be verified by hard evidence that it actually happened. Dr. Jim Tucker calls the cases that can be verified by tracing them to a person who actually lived as being "solved." Cases that cannot be traced to an actual deceased person are categorized as being unsolved. Dr. Tucker says about two-thirds of all the cases they have on file have been solved.

From the many books on cases of verified reincarnation I have in my library, I only have time and space for just one here. That is the case of James Leininger as recorded in the book "Soul Survivor" by his father and mother, Bruce and Andrea Leininger.

In the "Foreword" to the book, Carol Bowman writes:

> *The story of James Leininger is the best American case of a child's past life memory among the thousands I've encountered. It's extraordinary because little James remembers names and places from his past life that can be traced to real people and actual events—facts that can easily be verified. He was even reunited with people who knew him in his former life as a World War II pilot.*

And it is just that James Leininger remembers being a WW II pilot and getting shot down while on a bombing run over Chichi Jima. The story starts with James, near his second birthday, having nightmares and screaming, "Airplane crash! Plane on fire! Little man can't get out!"

A few days later, Andrea was pushing James in his stroller in downtown Lafayette Louisiana when they passed Hobby

Lobby, where an outside bin was filled with plastic toys. Andrea picked up a small propeller-driven plane. She handed it to James and stated, "And there's even a bomb on the bottom." Then James, this child still in diapers, turned the toy plane over and proclaimed, "That's not a bomb, Mommy. That's a dwop tank."

I will skip how the story develops and go straight to some of the verifiable details. James stated his ship had a name; it was "Natoma." He said he was a pilot also named James. His dad looked it up and found there was an aircraft carrier called the Natoma Bay CVE 62. A James Huston Jr. was on board who was shot down while on a bombing run over Chichi Jima.

James drew pictures of planes fighting and crashing. He always signed them "James 3". He said it was because he was the third James. That was before it was discovered that James Huston was a Jr. He said he had a buddy and a wingmate named Jack Larsen. It turned out that Jack Larsen was indeed a pilot on Natoma Bay. And Jack Larsen was still alive. They met Jack Larsen, who confirmed what James told them about Natoma Bay.

James said he had two sisters in his former life, Annie and Ruth, except he pronounced it "Roof." Anne was still alive and confirmed that only her dead brother called her Annie. James knew many details of their family life, which Anne. James asked about a portrait that their mother had painted of Anne. James asked about the portrait that no one else knew about. Anne retrieved the portrait from her attic and gave it to James.

James had three toy GI Joes that he named Billy, Leon, and Walter. Asked why he chose those names, James replied, "Because that's who met me when I got to heaven."

Bruce, James' father, looked up the names of the men who were killed on Natoma Bay. "Leon Conner was killed on October 25, 1944. Walter Devin on October 26, 1944. Billy Peeler was killed on November 17, 1944. James Huston was killed on March 3, 1945. Billy, Leon, and Walter were already dead and waiting for him when he got to heaven.

Note: The word "Heaven" is often used to refer to the place they go after death. They are not referring to a physical place, but it is the only word they know that just refers to the "other side."

Here I must tell a story of an experience I had with my oldest son, Rusty. Rusty is a materialist. I had given him my copy of "Soul Survivor." He read it and returned it to me. He now lives in Colorado, and I am in Alabama. I decided to call him and ask him about the case of James Leininger. I would remind him of all the very compelling evidence in the case. I had my ducks in a row. This was one debate I was going to win. Or at least I thought so at the time.

I briefly went over all the evidence, the drop tank, Jack Larsen, James' sister, the three GI Joes, and other evidence. I left him not one out. The evidence was overwhelming.

"Well," I asked him, "What do you think?"

He replied: "Err, this would mean they have souls."

"Well, yes," I replied.

Then came the five words that ended the debate. "I don't believe in souls."

56

I thought about this short debate for months. Why did the evidence simply make no difference whatsoever to Rusty? Then it came to me, I finally figured it out. The answer was so damn obvious that it hit me like a ton of bricks. When a person holds any belief or worldview as an absolute certainty, then any evidence that suggests that this worldview is incorrect is simply wrong; it is invalid. There cannot possibly be valid evidence that contradicts what one knows to be an absolute certainty. The evidence may look valid, and it may sound valid, but they know that if examined close enough and fact-checked meticulously, it will be found to be invalid. There can be no doubt about it. They don't even need to consider the evidence; it just has to be wrong. Case closed.

Just one more story, and I will move on. This is the only story I am personally acquainted with. Not exactly a reincarnation story, but strongly suggestive. This is an event given to me by a very dear lady friend of mine, whom I will call Lisa, as she asked me not to use her real name. Lisa was, at the time, about five years old. Her adoptive parents were Canadians living near Toronto. They were on vacation and driving through Bar Harbor, Maine, when Lisa suddenly developed an overwhelming desire to "see her house." She started screaming to her parents, "I want to see my house, I want to see my house." She described the house in detail and demanded to see it.

Exasperated, her parents decided they would have no peace until she got to see her house. She gave them directions. "Turn here, she would say until she led them to the house. It was exactly as she described it. "That's my house, that's my house," she shouted. Her parents were flabbergasted but had no explanation.

An important point about reincarnation I must point out here. Hypnotism is often used to regress people back to a past life. I believe this method of past-life inquiry is totally unreliable. The reason is the information received comes from the subconscious, or as often called, the unconscious mind. I have found, during my period as an amateur hypnotist, that the subconscious mind seems to have a strong desire to please whoever is making the inquiry. And as a result, the subconscious mind will just make up stuff. It will tell you damn lies. Of course, the subject under hypnosis has no control over what the subconscious mind is telling the hypnotist. I am not saying that all such cases are illegitimate, just that they are unreliable, and I never use them in my research.

Of course, every reported case of reincarnation cannot be verified. But if the phenomenon is to be taken seriously, then it must be verifiable. Dr. Ian Stevenson spent 40 years not just finding reincarnation cases but meticulously verifying each case's validity as well. Dr. Jim Tucker also makes strong efforts to verify each case he studies.

NDEs can often be verified by other evidence. Doctors, nurses, and others who witness such events testify that there was no other way the person could have otherwise known what they witnessed during the NDE. I have read of many hypnotic cases of past life regression, but not one that can be verified by hard evidence. But if I ever encounter one, I will certainly consider its legitimacy.

One more point on hypnotic regression. Some psychologists and other therapists use hypnotic regression, returning to a past life, to treat people with serious phobia problems. Such cases as an abnormal fear of water might be traced to the person drowning in a previous life. This is great if it cures their phobia. But unless the case can be traced back to an actual person who once lived, it cannot be used as proof of reincarnation.

Debunking the Debunkers

There are hundreds of books detailing the paranormal. They give us, in detail, cases of near-death experiences, out-of-body experiences, reincarnation, ESP, and many other such cases. Many books attempt to debunk all such arguments. But there I didn't have a single book in my library that attempts to debunk the debunkers. So I searched on Amazon.com for such a book. Then I thought I had found it. It was a book by Winston Wu titled: Debunking Pseudoskeptical Arguments of Paranormal Debunkers. I thought, "Hot damn, I have finally found one." I immediately purchased the Kindle book and dove into it. Here are a few examples of what I found in the first few pages:

> *When closed-minded cynicism comes masquerading as skepticism, it becomes a block to truth in finding an open-minded investigation.*

> *Pseudoskepticism is defined as thinking that claims to be Skeptical but is actually faith-based disbelief. Because real skepticism is a justifiable position, pseudoskepticism may also be defined as making pseudoscientific arguments in pursuit of a skeptical agenda.*

> *In truth and by their actions, these pseudoskeptics are defenders of the status quo and materialism. They are fanatics and dogmatists who have no regard for facts, evidence or truth but have an a priori faith-based belief that paranormal phenomena are impossible and therefore set out to debunk it, not investigate it. And they will distort, dismiss and*

obfuscate to get their way. Thus, they generally have no objectivity toward evidence, but bigotry and emotional fanaticism.

Then comes the "uh oh" killer paragraph on page 23.

If you're wondering if this is true, then ask yourself this: Why do those who attack, ridicule, and deny all paranormal claims also usually deny all conspiracies and facts in support of them while dogmatically accepting all propaganda by the media and establishment? Have you ever seen a paranormal debunker like James Randi, Michael Shermer, or CSICOP' Skeptical inquirer challenge anything official held by the status quo at all, period? If not, what does that tell you? Think about it.

I thought, "Oh shit, does that paragraph mean what I think it means. I then went to the website touted throughout the book: https://www.youtube.com/@SCEPCOP/videos. One video immediately caught my eye and was titled: "Navy Top Gun Questions Official 9/11 Story" Three more videos started off with the words "Moon Hoax," All videos that denied that we ever went to the moon. Dammit! I was so disappointed. I thought I had found an excellent book and an excellent website on debunking the debunkers. But it had a very serious flaw.

There were 38 YouTube videos on that site. I did not check them all, but the others I did check looked excellent. But I just could not get over the fact that the site promoted stupid conspiracy theories. I worked at NASA's George C. Marshall Space Flight Center for the last 17 years of my career. The moon landing was not a hoax. The thousands who worked on the project were not all lying. Again, if you

61

have a theory that requires thousands who say they have proof that your theory is wrong, then your theory is just wrong. Thousands cannot tell an outright, deliberate lie and keep it a secret.

Likewise, the theory that the events of September 11, 2001, were a U.S. Government false flag inside job is just damn stupid. Hundreds of engineers did not sneak into the Trade Center buildings and plant explosives. And if you watch the videos, you can plainly see that the collapse of both buildings begins at the floor of impact. Then they pancake down, one floor after another, all the way down. That would be impossible to do with explosives. How were the conspirators supposed to know which floor the planes would hit? And to believe that the hundreds who would have to have been in on the conspiracy would risk the death penalty if one of them ratted them out is… well… just beyond belief.

The rest of the book and the videos on the website are likely very good, though I have not watched them all. But the conspiracy nut-case theories just ruined it for me. To quote Dag Hammarskjold, "He who wants to keep his garden tidy does not reserve a plot for weeds."

Another good book is by Alex Tsakiris, "Why Science Is Wrong About Almost Everything." I don't like the title. The word "science" is simply a noun that refers to the study of the natural world. Scientists are often wrong, but saying they are wrong about almost everything is painting them with too broad a brush. I think they are right far more often than they are wrong.

Nevertheless, the book is an excellent read. Only in one other place did I find disagreement with Alex. That was the entire chapter he had on Darwin and evolution. He is a fan of Alfred Russel Wallace and says of him:

> *Wallace soon diverged or departed from Darwin's theory in proposing what I have referred to as "intelligent evolution," which is actually directed, detectably designed and purposeful common descent. In other words, there is teleology involved in certain aspects of evolution.*

However, I must disagree. I believe Darwin's theory of natural selection is all that is needed to drive evolution. As far as teleology (*intelligent design*) goes, as Laplace replied to Napoleon, "I have no need for that hypothesis." Of course, as I stated earlier, I believe some kind of conscious entity started it all. I think the recipe was written in the first instant of creation, and there was no need for that conscious being, or whatever it was, to fiddle with everything along the way.

I will just plug one other book, which I think may be the best of all. That is "Randi's Prize: What Sceptics Say About the Paranormal, Why They are *Wrong*" by Robert McLuhan. I don't like the title, however. Though Robert debunks James Randi's silly one-million-dollar prize, which Randi never intended to pay, that is only a very small part of the book. Though he takes 400 pages to do it, Robert McLuhan does a better job of debunking the debunkers than any other I have read.

Concerning the debunkers, there are charlatans just as in any field. Evolution has one very famous case. That is the case of the Piltdown Man. The Piltdown Man case was a fraud perpetrated in 1912 in which bone fragments were presented as the fossilized remains of a previously unknown early human. They were actually the cranium of a human and the jawbone of an orangutan with teeth that were filed down. It is a case that the creationists usually bring up when trying to debunk evolution. After all, it is one case that they can clearly show was a hoax.

The paranormal debunkers always pull the same trick. Of course, there are hoaxers out there. Those are the ones the debunkers always pick. They never choose to debunk the ones they cannot debunk. And if they do pick a hard one, they always pick the parts that they can shed doubt on, never the obvious events that cannot be explained. These, if they mention them at all, they just suggest deception on the part of those experiencing the event or reporting it.

One famous debunker is cosmologist Dr. Sean Carrol. I mentioned his book, The Big Picture: On the Origins of Life, Meaning, and the Universe Itself, earlier. In that book, he purports to settle the whole matter. He argues that not only that nothing exists except matter and energy because the laws of the material world just do not permit it. In the book, he, like other debunkers, picks only the easy and obvious cases. He debunks the spoon benders and the astrologers. Easy targets, anyway. He also attempts to debunk near-death experiences. There are, on file, thousands of NDE cases, though actual cases number in the millions. However, one case was clearly a hoax, an admitted hoax. That is the case of Alex Malarkey, as depicted in a book his father wrote, "The Boy Who Came Back from Heaven." That case is Dr. Carroll's Piltdown Man, the case he debunks and the only NDE he attempts to debunk.

Dr. Carroll makes bold statements that simply cannot be verified. Then he describes a truly absurd scientific test. On page 220, he says:

No case of claimed afterlife experiences have been subject to careful scientific protocols. People have tried; several studies have been conducted trying to find evidence for out-of-body experiences in patients who have near-death encounters. Researchers will visit hospital rooms and, without special knowledge on the part of patients or medical staff, hide some kind of visual stimulus in place where the patient would have to be floating freely out of their body to see it. To date, there have been no case where such a stimulus has been clearly seen.

What an unbelievable absurdity of a test? Someone who has a near-death, out-of-body experience while undergoing surgery, while in this state, even though they have no idea that some stimulus thingy had been hidden, they are still supposed to say to themselves: *"Now where did those scientists hide that stimulus thing I am supposed to find?"* Can you imagine anything so stupid? Yet, I have read of this test before. As absurd as such a test might seem, Dr. Carroll is not just making this up. They have actually done this. They are serious. They believe that because no one having an NDE has ever found their hidden stimulus, whatever that might have been, NDEs just don't happen. Dr. Carroll then states:

It's possible that the known laws of physics are dramatically wrong in such a way as to allow human consciousness to persist after the death of the physical body; however it is also possible that people under extreme conditions of nearly dying are likely to hallucinate, and that reports of prior lives are exaggerated or faked.

In classical logic, this is called the fallacy of begging the question or assuming the conclusion. It is assumed that if

65

paranormal phenomena exist, they must obey the laws of physics. That is, it must obey the laws of the material world. And since it does not obey the laws of the material world, the non-material world does not exist.

It never seems to occur to the debunkers to examine any of the thousands of NDEs, interview those who experienced them as well as those who witnessed them and were told of the things that they describe that would be impossible unless they actually had the experience they describe. I mean such cases as described by Dr. Bellg and Dr. Greyson in their books. Or the cases such as those described by Dr. Tucker and Dr. Stevenson in their books. Or the many other books where many other actual events are described by those who either experienced them or observed them. Then there are the other books that describe a single case that is so strong that it deserves a book of its own. Such a book as "Soul Survivor."

However, they would still have one out even if they did this. They could just say, "They are all lying." After all, that is what the flat earthers say. That is what the 9/11 truthers say. That is what those who claim the moon landing was a hoax say. And it seems to work for them. It just might work for those who claim all psychic phenomena are real and are lying as well.

Of course, that is faulty logic. One person may be lying, or even two dozen people may be lying. But a thousand people are not lying. I apologize for my tendency to keep hammering on this subject of lying. That is the most overlooked flaw in the debunker's argument. They completely overlook the fact that millions of people must be just outright lying about their experience if the materialist paradigm is true.

However, materialist faith that nothing exists outside the material world is so strong that they cannot possibly give up that belief. And it is faith, or just a belief because the nonexistence of anything cannot possibly be proven. But the existence of anything can be proven if it truly exists. It may not be proven by the test that you demand it pass to be proven, like the test of hiding something in a hospital and demanding that it be found or else NDEs you claim that NDEs do not exist. That's just a ploy, either it passes a test that you design or else it's invalid.

Either near-death experiences are real, or millions of people are lying. That is the test. There are not millions of cases of reincarnation, but the documented cases do number in the thousands. They are either valid, or they are all lying. The same goes for ESP and other psychic phenomena. They are genuine, or the many thousands of people who experienced and documented them are lying.

There is perhaps no better series of videos on PBS, and on YouTube, than the "Closer to Truth" series presented by Dr. Robert Lawrence Kuhn. There are hundreds of them, all related to science, consciousness, and the meaning of life. In one episode, titled "Is There Life After Death, Dr. Kuhn interviews two philosophers, two more "Christian" philosophers, A Rabbi who is also a Jewish philosopher, and a Buddhist Monk. Near the end of the video, Dr. Kuhn says:

> *"As for so-called evidence of an afterlife, I cannot imagine why if we do survive death, the evidence is so weak."*

Therein lies the rub. The evidence is not weak at all, the evidence is overwhelmingly strong. In another series titled "Do Persons Survive Death," Dr. Khun states:

Survival beyond death is at stake, and I am thumped by the stark antagonisms of the clashing positions. Science—no afterlife. Religion—big afterlife. Parapsychology—maybe some kind of afterlife. My head skews to science. My hope skirts to religion.

Another rub. Religion hasn't a damn thing to do with it. In fact, it is primarily because of religion that most scientists are so adamant that the survival of death is a myth. They know religion is a myth. Therefore the main tenant of religion, "survival of death" is also a myth. And who can blame them? Religion has a catch. That is that one must hold a certain belief, or else you don't get to inherit this everlasting life. And that, of course, is an antonym to common sense.

Therefore, according to religion, Dr. Kuhn has a problem. It seems he would just love to believe but just cannot, which means he will be left out of that heavenly roll call. Where he might wind up is another debate.

Regarding survival, in this series, Dr. Khun interviews well over forty scientists, philosophers, and theologians. He does interview a few, such as Charles Tart, Sam Parnia, and Stephen Browdy, who are more amenable to the subject. But the majority of his interviews were doubters or even overly hostile to the concept. One of his subjects was the late Robert Park, a former Physics Professor at the University of Maryland. In one video titled "What is an Afterlife," Professor Park states:

There's absolutely no reason to believe anything about an afterlife. Nobody comes back. Now and then, somebody claims to have come back. But none of this is ever verifiable. It's easy to make claims like that. And particularly a long time ago. So, nothing ever comes out of this. There is not a hint that is verifiable that there is an afterlife.

Professor Park goes on to state that it is used to manipulate people, which is, of course, correct. That is exactly what religion does, which is likely why so many scientists hate it so much. But he states that none of this is ever verifiable that bothers me. How does he know this?

Dr. Ian Stevenson spent 40 years studying reincarnation, meticulously verifying every case he studied. Dr. Jim Tucker, his successor at the University of Virginia, is doing the same thing. Verification is the main thrust of every case he studies.

Dr. Bruce Greyson, also at the University of Virginia, stresses verification in his near-death studies. If you read the many books and articles written by medical doctors like Dr. Lauren Bellg or cardiologists who have witnessed NDEs firsthand and testify to the things that their patients report that could not have possibly been known unless their out-of-body experience was real, then you will understand just how strongly these phenomena have been verified.

But why do some scientists and philosophers insist that there has been no verification whatsoever of any paranormal phenomena? Though they have never studied the over 2,000 cases of verified reincarnation on file at the University of Virginia, Department of Perceptual Studies. Nor have even bothered to look at the many thousands of cases and studies on file at Cambridge University, Society for Psychical Research. And I could name a dozen other Universities or Institutions that engage in such studies and have, in their files, verified cases of NDEs, reincarnation, or other cases of paranormal phenomena. Why?

It took me years to finally figure it out, I now know exactly why they never even bother to look at the overwhelming amount of verified evidence held by these institutions. It is because they think they know, with absolute certainty, that any paranormal phenomenon is impossible. They believe, like Sean Carroll, that the laws of physics are so tight that they rule out ESP forever. They know, with absolute certainty, that the material world is all that exists. Therefore, it is a total waste of time to examine any so-called evidence because it cannot exist. Or so they believe. They have declared that nothing has been verified without even attempting to check for verification of anything.

As I wrote earlier, they are no different from me in that regard. Examining any evidence presented to me that the earth is flat is a waste of time. But I have already examined the overwhelming evidence that the earth is a globe. They, on the other hand, have not examined any evidence held by the over a dozen universities and institutions that the evidence of paranormal phenomena is legitimate and verifiable.

The debunkers try not to examine the evidence to see if it is legitimate but just to assume that the evidence is illegitimate and debunk it. A perfect example of this behavior by the debunkers can be found in those recently trying to debunk the psychic medium Matt Fraser.

First, let me say that there are phony psychic mediums. Every medium is different in their ability to perform. Some have enormous talent, like Matt Frasier, and some have no psychic ability. And there are many who range somewhere

70

between those two extremes. So, people are justified in being skeptical about psychic mediums because some are indeed fakes. But all are not.

One group of skeptics advertised online for volunteers to debunk Matt Fraser. Here is their Reddit ad.

> *We are looking for people who are willing to participate in the exposing of grief vampire Matt Fraser.*

They wanted to expose him as a fake. Obviously, what he was telling his subjects, which were often just members of an audience for shows he was a guest on, was accurate and valid. So, they felt he had to get his data in advance. But how? Since the audience did not fill out questionnaires as some faith healers require, he must be using another method. Facebook, they surmised, he must be getting his information from Facebook. So, they had members of their group fill out fake Facebook profiles. They used fake names and posted about fake deceased family members. Then they attended a show where Fraser would perform. But alas, Fraser never gave any of them a reading, so their efforts were a total bust.

It seems the height of absurdity to think that Matt Fraser gets his information from scanning thousands of Facebook profiles, memorizing them, then being able to pick them from the audience of the shows in which he appears. But they knew, with absolute certainty, that he was faking it. His readings were just too accurate, so he had to be getting his information illegitimately. Facebook was the only place they could imagine, so they went with that.

I believe Matt Fraser is legitimate. I have only one problem with him. I just wish he wouldn't think he needs to dress like Liberace.

Conclusion

A new scientific truth does not triumph by convincing its opponents and making them see the light, but rather because its opponents eventually die, and a new generation grows up that is familiar with it. – Max Planck

The above Max Planck quote is known as "Planck's Principle and has been translated into: "Science advances one funeral at a time." In other words, most scientists are locked into their worldviews. And those worldviews state that it's a materialist universe, and any suggestion that it is not is nothing but religious superstition and should be ignored. And they will, very likely, hold that worldview until the day they die.

That is not just the case for scientists but philosophers, psychologists, neurologists, and members of the new atheist movement. A person's worldview is who they are. To change one's worldview is to admit that they have been wrong all their life. And that is damn nearly impossible to do. That would be a blow to the ego too difficult to bear. So, the evidence of the existence of any kind of spiritual world must be ignored. Not just ignored, but it must be declared outright that any verifiable evidence of the paranormal doesn't exist.

That was the unofficial scientific paradigm throughout the twentieth century. Of course, people had near-death experiences, children reported remembering their past life, people had out-of-body experiences, and mediums practiced their trade. However, it was mostly hushed up. People never talked about their NDE, and when children spoke of their

72

other mothers and how they died, they were told to shut up and stop talking nonsense. But that has all changed.

Now we have what is called "social media." And the most effective form of social media is something called YouTube. People, via YouTube, are learning about a world they never knew existed. They are learning about the millions of NDEs, and hundreds of them are detailed on YouTube videos by the people who experienced them. They are learning of the many cases of small children remembering their past life. Information about the spiritual world is exploding.

If psychic phenomena are ever to be generally accepted, then only that which can be verified should be part of the story. Anything that must be accepted on faith makes it just like religion. Near-death experiences must be verified. Children remembering past lives must be verified. Medium readings must be verified. Things that cannot possibly be verified must be eschewed like the plague. These include online astrologers, tarot card readers, and others who will tell your future for a price. It is likely a grift if there is no way to validate their work. Then there are the biggest grifters of all, the so-called physical mediums who operate in dark rooms and claim to be able to produce a ghostly material called ectoplasm from the orifices of their body.

But how do we know that which we claim to be verified is really verified? We know for the same reason we know that the earth is a globe. We know because all those who claim to have the evidence are not liars. It is said that three people can keep a secret as long as two of them are dead. A thousand people cannot tell the same lie and keep it a secret. The thousands of people who worked on the moon landing are not lying. The millions of people who claim to have had a near-death experience are not lying when they tell of things

73

they could not possibly have known unless they experienced exactly what they claim. The thousands of small children and their parents are not lying when they tell of their experiences that can be traced to actual deceased people and tell of events in these people's lives that can be verified.

Again, if you have a worldview that requires the thousands to millions who claim to have contrary evidence to be outright liars, then your worldview is just wrong, damn wrong.

Regardless of what some scientists and philosophers are telling us that is impossible, people continue to have near-death experiences, and children continue to report their past life. But now those who report their experience of an NDE or the child who speaks of his or her former life ate listened to instead of being told they are hallucinating. More and more of these NDEs and cases of reincarnation will be reported on social media. They will become totally commonplace instead of shunned as hallucinations or just lies. The dam has broken, and there is no way the debunkers and deniers can possibly stop it.

Of course, this will make absolutely no difference to the hard-core materialist. After all, they know, with absolute certainty, that psychic phenomena are impossible. They know that there are no such things as souls. But, as Max Planck said, science advances one funeral at a time. These die-hard materialists will eventually die, and a new generation that is familiar with the evidence of the non-material world grows up.

Nevertheless, I have hope that a few of them allow reason, logic, evidence, and common sense to reshape their worldview. Well, some hope, but not a lot.

74

Made in United States
Orlando, FL
19 July 2023

35273694R00043